Eric's
Greek Travel Diary

by

Eric

With help from
Louise Schofield (story) and
Rae Dale (illustrations)

KEEP OUT!
(That means you)

Rigby PM Collection and PM Plus

Sapphire Level 30

U.S. Edition © 2013 HMH Supplemental Publishers
10801 N. MoPac Expressway
Building #3
Austin, TX 78759
www.hmhsupplemental.com

Text © 2003 Cengage Learning Australia Pty Limited
Illustrations © 2003 Cengage Learning Australia Pty Limited
Originally published in Australia by Cengage Learning Australia

12   1957   14
19190

Text: Louise Schofield
Illustrations: Rae Dale
Printed in China by 1010 Printing International Ltd

Eric's Greek Travel Diary
ISBN 978 0 75 786930 3

Contents

Chapter 1

Flying

It's Aunt Matilda's fault. Here I am on a plane to Greece and NOT at my best friend's birthday sleepover, which is happening at this very moment.

I really wanted to be there. I promised I'd tell the ghost stories at midnight. My stories are always the scariest, and Pete is FANTASTIC at the sound effects.

But now nobody will be scared, and Pete's party will be just a party.

I've let my friend down.

It's Aunt Matilda's fault alright.

She's the one who told Mom about Athens and the island of Crete. About "ancient temples and fascinating artifacts." About "quaint fishing ports and delicious food." She can be very convincing.

One time Matilda talked Mom into taking me on a trek through Nepal, even though I begged her to leave me behind. I survived that trip pretty well (Nepal was a cool kind of place), but this time there is no doubt in my mind.

I'd rather be with Pete!

Oh well, there's nothing I can do about it now, so ... I'll ask for another juice and settle down to watch the movie. I think it's a good one.

I wonder what's for dinner. What will be in those little plastic boxes? I wonder what they're having at the party ...

(Mrs. Smith, my teacher, asked me to keep a diary of the trip. I'll write more later.)

Chapter 2

Athens and the Ancients

We're at our hotel in Athens now. Athens is the capital of Greece. It's been a busy day.

When we arrived last night, we could see the ruins of the Acropolis (Uh-cro-pol-lis) lit up on a hill above the city. So today, that was the first place Mom and I wanted to visit.

We got out our guidebook, checked the map, and off we went ...

The Acropolis is the name of the area on top of this flat hill above Athens, and boy, does it have some old stuff up there! Thousands of years old!

The Parthenon is this huge temple with lots of stone columns. It's an amazing building and it used to contain one of the Seven Ancient Wonders of the World — a 40 foot gold and ivory statue of the goddess Athena. The statue was stolen a long time ago.

Who is Athena?

According to my guidebook, Athena was the Greek goddess of war and wisdom (and a few other things). The Romans called her Minerva.

The owl is her sacred bird, which is why owls are associated with learning. Her dad was called Zeus (Zoo-ss). He was the king of the gods.

There's a story that explains why Athens was named after her, and it goes like this:

Athena and Poseidon (Pos-eye-don), the god of the sea, were competing to become patron of a new city (a patron takes care of something). To show his power, Poseidon struck his trident (spear) on the rock of the Acropolis. It opened and water gushed out. Great party trick!

In reply Athena struck the ground with a rod and created the first olive tree. She was chosen, and so the city was named after her.

Mom says that olives are very important to the Greeks for food and oil. So I guess they made the right decision ...

Another of the important buildings at the Acropolis is the Erechteum (E-reck-tee-oom) where both Athena and Poseidon are honored.

You can't go into the old buildings anymore, but apparently inside the Erechteum there is a rock with the holes made by Poseidon's trident. It's said that when the wind blows south you can hear the sea.

We also saw the famous group of columns called the Caryatid Porch (Kari-atid), where ladies hold up the roof with their heads! Ouch!

After the Acropolis, Mom and I wandered down the hill into Plaka (Plark-uh), which is a maze of narrow alleys and winding stairs, shops, and restaurants.

I was starving, so we found a place to eat lunch. First I noticed there was octopus on the menu. No way was I going to eat octopus! Can you imagine what that would be like? Mom says it's delicious, but I don't believe her.

We settled on souvlakis (soov-lark-ees) with salad. Souvlaki is little pieces of meat on a skewer, grilled with herbs and stuff, and served with bread that looks like a pancake. Yum!

On the way back to our hotel we passed a market. Mom bought some beads from a man at a stall. She said they are called worry beads, and you "play" with them when you're worried or thinking about something important. They are made out of amber, which is the *fossilized sap* of ancient trees. These beads are a mix of golden yellow and red — Mom thinks they're beautiful.

Maybe I need some worry beads. I'm still worried that Pete will be mad at me for missing his party! Maybe he won't be my best friend anymore.

Chapter 3

The Golden Mask

Wow! What a day! Today we went to the National Archaeological Museum. It has some amazing stuff!

A lot of Greece's treasure has been stolen or wrecked over the years. The things left are now protected in museums like this one. We saw lots of golden treasure and tons of ancient pottery, as well as statues and wall paintings, including some from the Acropolis.

All of it was very old.

We both liked the statue of the Jockey of Artemision (Art-e-mizz-ee-on). He was riding a horse — FAST!

I really liked the gold death mask of Agamemnon (Aga-mem-non). He was a king who lived more than 3,500 years ago.

The mask would look great on my bedroom door.

This is the gigantic bronze statue of Poseidon. He's about to throw his trident.

I've put a sticker on him, Mrs. Smith, so you won't be embarrassed. Mom says you won't be, as it is classical art, but I wanted to be sure.

Tomorrow we will take a boat ride to Crete (Creet). Crete is the biggest island in Greece. I can hardly wait, but I wish Pete was with us.

Chapter 4

Off
to the Islands

Yassou Pete! (hello in Greek)

Mom and I are in a great Internet cafe not far from our hotel. We've had a great time in Athens, and we've seen some awesome things.

This afternoon we will ride on a bus to the port, where we'll get on an overnight ferry to Crete.

I hope your party was SCARY without me. I feel really bad about missing it, but I promise to pick you up something special as a present.

Say hi to everyone for me! And tell Mrs. Smith that I'm writing in my diary every day. Wish you were here (you, not Mrs. Smith!).

See ya! :-)

Chapter 5

Eric's Decision

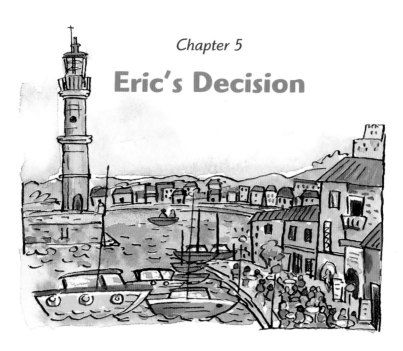

The ferry trip to Crete was great! We slept in deck chairs and woke up at sunrise as we entered the port. We caught a bus to Chania (Harn-ee-uh), the capital, then cruised on down to its old fishing harbor.

Mom says the old part of the city is Venetian. There are fantastic cobblestone streets with all kinds of buildings squashed together — nice and cozy. Some buildings are in ruins, but they look kind of good.

Our hotel overlooks the port.

This afternoon we avoided the waterfront area full of tourists and walked to the beach.

On the way back we heard Greek music and smelled wonderful food smells. Under some trees beside the road was a "kantina," a kind of kitchen on wheels. There were tables scattered around and lights hung from the branches. We sat at a table, and a smiling old man who couldn't speak English served us some dips with toasted bread. We ate it with Greek salad.

Greek salad has lettuce, feta cheese, tomatoes, and olives in it. Feta cheese is white and salty.

As the sun set, some Greek men began playing backgammon at one of the tables. Mom and I watched them play as they sipped on their drinks.

We decided this place was better than the expensive restaurants on the waterfront. It was real Greece, not just a place for tourists. And it was here that I made a decision.

I would learn how to play the national game of Greece. I would buy a backgammon set for Pete and then teach him how to play, too. Pete loves new games.

Chapter 6

The Search is Fruitful

Today we explored the back streets of Chania. I love the colors of the houses and doors. We took lots of photos!

We saw a shop that sells different types of olives. Mom tasted them and bought a bag of the ones she liked best. (The black ones are the ripe fruit.)

I finally found a backgammon set for Pete. I bought one for me and Mom to use, too. After dinner we read the rules and played our first game.

I won!

Chapter 7

The
Long Gorge

Am I tired! It's the end of a long day, but it was fun.

Before sunrise Mom and I rode on a bus that took us up into the White Mountains. We got off the bus with lots of other people, just as the sun came up.

We were about to hike through one of the longest gorges in Europe, the Gorge of Samaria. This gorge is 8 miles long, and the trail to the coast is another two miles.

We followed a beautiful stream downhill. The water was a clear turquoise color because of the white rocks underneath.

Mom and I walked through rocky areas where wild goats live, and later passed the ruins of the Samaria village. The narrowest part of the gorge is just a few feet wide, but 1,000 feet high. This is known as The Iron Gate.

Walking here reminded us of our hike in Nepal, although in the Himalayas we walked for days, not just hours ... Just as well, because toward the end of our gorge walk, Mom slipped and twisted her ankle.

Luckily another walker was passing by and had a bandage in her backpack. Someone else loaned Mom his walking stick.

At last we reached the end of the trail, the village of Agia Roumeli (Arg-ee-uh Roo-mel-ee), which looks over the Libyan Sea. After getting something to eat, we rode in a boat and then on a bus back to Chania.

I was tired, and Mom's ankle was sore, but after dinner we still managed to play a game of backgammon.

Mom won this time. It made her feel much better!

Chapter 8

Climbing the Minaret

In the morning, Mom and I packed our bags and rode on a bus to Rethimnon (Re-thim-non), which is on the coast east of Chania. We checked into a hotel near the beach, and after lunch we walked slowly to the top of a Turkish minaret — a really tall tower. It had a great view of the sea, the port, the beach, and a fort on top of a hill nearby. Mom's ankle was much better.

Chapter 9

Humiliated

Rethimnon's old Venetian fort is surrounded by a high stone wall that you can see from most parts of the city. We took a taxi ride to the fort after breakfast, before the day got hot.

Inside the fort were stone buildings that had been built later by the Turkish people. There is an underground water reservoir there as well.

Later, Mom and I went swimming at the beach to cool off.

Today I tried dolmades (doll-mar-dez). Dolmades are vine leaves stuffed with rice and other foods. At first I wasn't sure about them, but after one, I wanted more!

Naturally, we had to play backgammon after dinner. This time we took my set down to a restaurant and played on a table there. We played two games this time. Mom won both!

(This is most embarrassing, especially because I lost in a public place. I hope to win tomorrow.)

Chapter 10

Three Reasons for Iraklion

We rode on a bus to Iraklion (Ir-ak-leon), which is a big port city. We're here for three things. The first is to visit the nearby Minoan palace of Knossos (Noss-oss) — we're going there tomorrow. The second is to check out Iraklion's Archaeological Museum. We went there this afternoon. (Mom LOVED the Minoan gold jewelry.)

The third reason for being here is to catch the boat back to Athens, so I can go home and play backgammon with Pete.

Tonight I won the first game. Unfortunately, Mom won the next game and is maintaining her lead.

Chapter 11

The
Palace of Knossos

Mom and I got on an early bus to Knossos. It was good to wander through with only a few other tourists around.

Knossos is more than 4,000 years old! It's a huge Minoan palace complex, dug up by archaeologists at the beginning of the last century.

Part of Knossos has been restored to make it look like it once did, with murals on the walls and huge painted columns. The pictures reminded me of Egyptian paintings. You know, where the people stand sideways, in profile.

Tonight Mom and I talked about everything we'd seen at Knossos, while we played our last games of backgammon. I've finally got the hang of it.

I won the first game and almost lost the second. But then I captured one of her last pieces and held her until I was unbeatable!

The ferry leaves for Athens in the morning, and then we'll be flying home. As soon as I get back, I'm going to see Pete.

Chapter 12

Sweet Defeat

HOME

Mrs. Smith, I know I haven't written in my diary for a few days. Sorry about that, but I can tell you what happened after we got home.

Pete loved his backgammon set. We played a game while we sipped our favorite drinks and ate dolmades Mom had bought from the deli.

Pete won! And guess what — I didn't mind one bit. He's the best friend ever!

THE END